DEDICATION

This book is dedicated to the young people of today who think that being thirty is old, forty is really old, and fifty is basically like having one foot in the grave.

I cherish your view of the world!

What to expect in - Reaching The Peak

1

Almost There

You're almost there! This book is called "Reaching the peak" because you are almost to the place where you desire to be, the end of this book!

I know, it's a lot of words! But stick with me! You might be getting tired. You might wonder if it's all worth it. You might even wonder what else there could possibly be.

Let me assure you, it's all going to be worth it!

I want to warn you about this section. Just like when you reach the peak of a real mountain, the terrain gets more technical, so is this book. This is not a race, it's a steady climb. Each page of this final book of Your Journey Of Being A Teenager is going to bring you one step closer to the peak. From there, you will see everything with clarity.

The most important part of this book is the understanding of the information. Yes, I may get more technical, and the diagrams might look boring or confusing right now, but it's actually really fun!

Once you understand this stuff, you will be able to live your life in a way that very few people ever do. You will live life in the moment! You will love your life for what it is! You will be a life designer!

That doesn't mean you are a professional life design expert though, because in order to be a professional, you have to earn money from it.

For now, just take this last section, step by step! You're above the clouds now! It's time to start enjoying the view of what's possible in your life. If you need help at any time, I'm here to help you!

If you get confused, re-read the chapter you just read, and then think about how it actually works in your life.

Watch, as all this information comes together and you begin to see exactly why all this stuff matters in your life.

I'm extremely proud of you for reaching this point, and I'm also extremely humbled by the fact that you made it this far.

2

I'm Humbled

Have you ever noticed how some adults seem to think they know it all? Do you ever feel like they see themselves as better than you, smarter than you, and more capable than you? I do! Even today, I see it in my own life. IT'S ANNOYING!

Personally, I won't do that to you, for the simple fact that I realize I'm not smarter than you. I, much like you, am just doing my best to live the best life I can live. My only reason for writing this book is to introduce you to some ideas that I've had throughout my lifetime, that I hope somehow improve your life.

To be honest, I'm completely humbled that you are even still reading this book. That would be the same as you wanting to sit in my classroom, and listen to me talk for hours! EEEWWW, when I put it that way, it doesn't sound like such a good idea after all.

The biggest difference is this. My classroom is the world around you! My hope is that when you go through life, every moment of it, that something I've said will help you. I hope that my voice inspires you to go out into this world and do extraordinary things!

I don't want any credit for your success. I had nothing to do with it. If you choose to use what you have, and are about to learn, to go out into this world and make a major impact, doing what YOU think is important, that's awesome!

I'm just a guy doing the same thing. My personal goal is to make a major impact in your life, and in the world, so that when my time is up, I'll leave the world with my own sense of inner peace.

I hope I inspire you! I hope I motivate you! I hope I give you hope, courage, inspiration, a vision of what is possible, and a sense of purpose for your life! That is what I want to BE in your life.

The reason I am so humbled, is because it's not me, it's YOU, who has allowed me to be in your life. That brings me to my knees, and humbles me to the point of feeling blessed beyond belief.

You see, I believe that I've been given a gift. The gift I'm referring to is writing. It's my art form, and I use it to paint a picture of possibility. If you can see a new vision of what is possible for your life, when you are done reading this book, I will feel as though I've done my J.O.B. well!

My Journey Of Being, is to BE the person who leads you to the place you want to be in your life. If you'll allow me to do that…..Thank you.

3

It's TIME

There is a famous sports announcer who gets me excited every time I hear him say "IT'S TIME!" He says it with such enthusiasm, such passion, and so much excitement, that I really believe that he is truly loving the fact that this moment has arrived.

I'm here to tell you the same thing, and if you would, imagine me saying it with the amount of enthusiasm that he has. I'm not just saying it, I'm feeling it, I'm experiencing and living it as if it's the most important moment of our entire lives! You, and me, in this moment!

Imagine a stadium full of people, ready to see the best event they've ever experienced! The energy is out of control, the people are amped up, and the crowd is ready to see what they've been waiting for their whole life! This moment, this one event, this spectacular time in your life is everything you have ever wanted it to be, and now....

"iiiiiiiiiiiittttttttsssssss TIME!!!!!"

I want to start having some real fun with this! I hope you've been having fun already, however, NOW, is the moment I've been excited to introduce you to. This moment, is the moment you've been waiting for! This moment is the exact moment in your life, when everything happens, everything matters, and everything is going to change! This moment is the only moment that matters, in your entire life! This moment is the moment your entire life has been leading up to. THIS IS YOUR MOMENT, THIS IS YOUR TIME!

"Huh? Really Tom? I'm literally just sitting here, reading your book. It's not as exciting as you might think it is. Seriously dude, take a chill pill!"

Alright, maybe I am a bit excitable. But that is how I like to live life! I only get one shot at this, and to me, this moment is the greatest moment of life.

Think about it, what else do you have? You've had a lot of moments in your life already, however, you don't have those moments any more except in memory.

You aren't guaranteed tomorrow, the next day, or even later today. Of course we always look forward to those times, yet we never know what will happen between right now, and then.

So what are you left with? You have THIS MOMENT! This finite particle of time, in the exact place where you are right now, IS YOUR LIFE!

My job is to help you to make the best of every moment of your life. Too many people waste the moments of their life, viewing them as nothing special, nothing to enjoy, nothing to celebrate, and nothing to appreciate. When in fact, this very moment of your life is the exact thing you should be celebrating, appreciating, enjoying and viewing as the most important moment of your life! It's the only one you have, and this moment is the only one you will EVER have!

4

What is a moment

So, what exactly is a moment? Is it a specific period of time? Is it a minute? Is it a second? Is it a millisecond? Is it a day? YES!

Think about this, on the timeline of forever, your life will come and go in a matter of moments. If your life was placed on the timeline of eternity, it would not even seem to exist. Your life, as depressing as it sounds, is nothing more than a short moment in time where you will be here one moment and gone the next.

Ouch, that's a harsh thing to say, isn't it.

Here is what I want you to understand about all this "Moment" stuff though. Moments matter! Every moment matters! What you do in the moment matters, because moments are opportunities for action, and once an opportunity passes by, the moment you could have taken action is over.

I'm going to show you some things, that might just blow your mind about life. Let me apologize in advance if you have a difficult time understanding why the world is the way it is, after you read this book.

To be honest, I view life a bit differently. I see it as a story to be told, with people as the actors and a constantly evolving stage that changes in every moment. This story as I see it, is told by us, and we get to choose the ending. If you consider the fact, that all stories have a beginning, a middle, and an end, why would life be any different?

So I want to invite you to look at life differently with me from now on. See life as a series of moments and believe that in each moment you have the ability to CREATE YOUR LIFE! It's all one big pattern, and you get to decide how the final design looks.

When you are finished with this book, you will understand more than most adults understand. You will be able to do more than most adults do, and you will be able to believe in a possibility that most adults don't.

There is going to be one big difference between you, and the rest of the world in regards to what you understand about life. What you choose to do with what I'm going to teach you will be the only thing that sets you apart in a world where people are supposed to be "Normal."

Will you choose to go out into this world and make an impact that creates waves, large enough to alter the landscape of the entire world? Or, will you play small, and barely move a feather?

The choice is yours! Because right now, you have the choice, this moment, and the possibility of doing anything you believe is possible!

I believe in you! I believe in your ability to actually do something amazing with your life! I believe that if you apply what you are learning in this book, to your everyday life, that your life will be extraordinary every day!

5

The three things

In your lifetime, you will only ever have three things.

You have, right now, This moment, a choice, and possibility!

What I mean by that is in this exact moment of your life, literally, right now, you can choose anything you want. If you want to choose to stop reading, you can do that. If you want to choose to keep reading, you can do that too.

If you want to choose to go to the moon, you can choose that also. Do you want to become a famous movie star? Choose to do it. Do you want to win an Olympic gold medal? Choose that too!

When you make the choice, you also have the possibility of it happening, or not. Just because you choose it, doesn't mean it will happen. Whether or not you get to be, do, or have what you choose depends on what you've already learned.

If you choose to go to the moon, all that separates you from that goal is your actions, your belief in it being possible, and your consistency. It's up to you to make it happen.

The ABC's of success, and time, are the only things separating you from anything you choose.

I'm going to start drawing some things for you, so you begin to really understand what you are learning.

This is the pattern of our life. It's called an equilateral triangle.

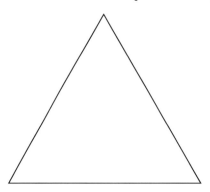

If you remember, from the ABC's of success, the bottom of the triangle represents the starting point, and the top of the triangle is the peak. Your belief is at the bottom, your goal is at the top, and when your actions and your consistency meet at the top, that is the moment when you will have what you want.

Here is how that looks.

Pretty simple right? You begin at the bottom, you take consistent actions, based in the belief that you can get there, and eventually, you wind up at the top of the mountain, being what you want to be.

Now that you understand the pattern of life, I'm going to break it down into smaller pieces. The smallest thing you have is this moment. It's literally an infinitesimal (big word that means really, really small) point in your life.

A moment is right now, right now, and…. Wait for it…… right now. Moments are all you ever have.
Moments are what this entire book is about. Moments are the most important thing in your life, because once you run out of moments…..you're…… I think you get the idea.

In the amount of time it takes to snap your finger, everything in life can change. So the choices you make in each of your moments are extremely important because they determine the direction your life goes.

This is the basis of the entire pattern of life. Everything is based off this one simple thing. The center of the X is the moment of choice, it always has been, and it always will be. Yes, I used the word always:

Like you learned, in the ABC's of Success, your belief is what determines the direction you go. If you have a positive belief, your life will move in one direction, if you have a negative disbelief, your life moves in another direction.

Here is how that looks:

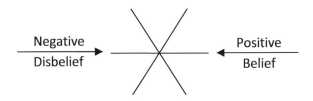

The reason your life moves in a certain direction, based on your belief is because in the moment, we only have the three most important things you'll ever have.

Moment – Choice – Possibility

In this and every moment you have the choice of what to believe, and in this moment, ANYTHING is possible. As long as you understand that every moment, literally every split second of life, also contains a choice, that is what I want you to understand.

If you are a little confused, don't worry about it. Nothing is wrong! Just remember those three words…. moment, choice, possibility.

Got it?

Good!

6

Negative disbeliefs

What are negative disbeliefs? They are the most devastating beliefs you can have in your life. Negative disbeliefs are the very thing that set you on a path of darkness.

Negative disbeliefs are what keep you living in the shadows of the dark clouds of your own **Fear**, **Influence**, **Reasons**, and **Emotions**. Those dark clouds are full of what holds you back. That space is run by "The Darkness" and it's the darkness's job to ruin your life!

Imagine if you will, that plankton we talked about earlier, is a real thing. That thing is an invisible force that walks the earth, looking for its next victim. It's always awake, it never rests, and it's on a journey of being your worst enemy! That's its J.O.B. in life!

The unfortunate part of this thing is that because you can't see it it's able to sneak up to you, find your weakness, and use it to keep you down. Sometimes, that bucket of water you use to splash in the face of the negative words it speaks are enough to get it to go away, but other times you need something more powerful. I'm going to tell you about a larger weapon in a little while.

So imagine that dark force, standing about three fourths of the way up the mountain. Around it, are those dark clouds of doom. It generates those clouds because it is so evil, that no light lives within it. It's mean, ugly, vial, and it wants nothing more than to see you living the worst life you can ever imagine.

When you are feeling weak, helpless, unhappy, angry, disgusted, or any other negative emotion, it is happy.

When you are feeling negative, it's looking at you, mocking you, and laughing at you! It loves to tell you things like "You CAN'T do it! You'll NEVER succeed! You

ALWAYS fail! Don't even TRY to do that again!"

I hope that your lip is curling at the idea of this thing even existing, yet it does. It's real, it's out there, and it wants to destroy all that is good in this world.

I want you to develop a real sense of this thing. If you are feeling any way other than pure joy in life, understand that the darkness is what is causing you to feel that way.

The darkness causes you to start having negative disbeliefs! NEGATIVE DISBELIEFS are a vital part of this book, so please remember that term.

7

Positive beliefs

The opposite of darkness is what? LIGHT! So if you are ever feeling held down by the F.I.R.E. of life, then you'll need to look for the light in order to get back to where you want to be.

The light, lives in the exact opposite place as the darkness. The darkness lives below you, the light lives above you.

What happens, many times, is that something can be going well for us, and at that time, we feel happy, positive, appreciative, and loving. When we feel that way we feel light, like anything is possible and like nothing can hold us back! That is how I want you to feel ALL THE TIME!

So if the light lives above you, and the darkness lives below you, then where do you need to focus your attention? You need to focus your attention on keeping your head up, looking toward the peak, while being aware of the fact that the darkness wants to trip you up every chance it gets.

Imagine for a minute, that you just won a BIG race! You are feeling VICTORY like you have never experienced before. How would your arms and hands be positioned? They would be held high, above your head, stretched out wide with your eyes toward the sky. You would probably even say "YES! THANK YOU!" and in that moment, you would feel like nothing could touch you and you could not be defeated.

That is how the light wants you to feel at all times! The light, is always there for you, always able to meet you in the exact place you are, even when you feel like you are in total darkness.

The light, is infinitely more powerful than the darkness. In fact darkness doesn't actually have any power, because darkness is nothing more than the absence of light. However, the light is always present, The only time you may feel like it's not, is when you are focused on the darkness, which is below you.

You can practice this by sitting, right now, and literally just thinking about good and bad. Think of something good, you feel light. Think of something bad, you feel dark.

This is ALL going to make complete sense to you soon. For now, as long as you understand that difference between the darkness and the light, that is all you need to know.

8

The Focus

What you focus on expands. The thing you look at is what you focus on. You don't need eyes to focus either. You can focus your thoughts just the same as you can focus your eyes, or the lens of a camera.

For example. Right now, think of something that makes you feel really horrible. It can be a person, a place, an activity, something that happened to you, or anything else. Just really FOCUS on that negative thing.

How do you feel when you focus on that thing? Do you feel heavy? Does it feel like a darkness is upon you? Does it feel like you are unable to move freely because something is holding you back? Do you feel like you want to escape but you're not sure how?

THAT IS THE DARKNESS!

By focusing on the negative disbelief, you begin to feel held down. Like everything that happens to you could cause you to fall further and further into the dark pit of despair. That is NOT a fun place to be!

Now, focus on something you absolutely LOVE! It can be anything! You choose what to focus on, just make sure it's something that makes you feel pure JOY!

How do you feel now? Do you feel light? DO you feel like you are free, like this is the place you want to live in?

THAT IS THE LIGHT!

I want you to be perfectly clear about understanding what it was that caused you to feel those feelings. It was YOUR FOCUS! You can only focus on one thing at a time. Our actual visual focal point is so small, that everything beyond that pin point focal view is blurry.

Do it with your eyes now. Focus on something in front of you, and really become aware of how small your actual focus point is. It's finite, which means really, really small. Sure you can see a lot, but you are only able to focus on a very small point.

Every time you focus, you are experiencing a new moment. So now that you understand focus, take your eyes and move them around the room. Each time you focus on something new, understand that you are focusing on that new thing, in a new moment.

Every moment brings with it a new opportunity to focus on something. What you CHOOSE to focus on, is what determines where you go.

From now on, I want you to be really clear about what it means to be focused on something.

When you are focused on something, you see it clearly. When you are focused on something, you are unable to focus on anything else. Focus can help you get where you want to be, and focus can hold you back.

Where you are, and where you go, all depends on where your focus is.

So now, you understand what a moment is, and you understand what focus is, right?

Great! I knew you were a fast learner!

9

It's Your Choice

Since you have the opportunity in each new moment to focus on anything you want to focus on, then what do you actually have? You have a choice!

Choice is the other thing you have in the moment. You get to choose.

Darkness or light

Happy or sad

Good or bad

Say something nice or say something mean

Be loving or be hateful

This or that

You choose!

Literally everything you ever do in your life is the result of a choice you make in the moment of choice.

To illustrate this, look at what is near you. Do you see two objects that you could pick up? Whatever two things you can pick up, I want you to choose one and pick it up.

Did you do it? Great!

Now, put it back down, and choose again.

Did you do it? Did you choose the same one, or did you choose a different one?

Either way, you made the choice, and you took the action.

Before you chose, you decided. Decision is not the factor that determines where your life goes, choice is!

The moment of choice is the moment you take action.

This is an ongoing cycle of life. It is the pattern that determines where you ultimately wind up. In fact, every choice you have ever made in your life, has brought you to *THIS* exact moment *RIGHT NOW!*

You are stuck with this pattern of life, so I'm going to suggest that you choose to start accepting it, and using it to your advantage.

If I told you something was possible, and someone else told you it was not possible, who would you believe?

You would probably go through a decision process, and then make your choice. That is what we do. You would make the choice based on what you believe.

So what if one of those things was a positive belief, and one of those things was a negative disbelief? Which one would you choose?

Obviously, you would probably say the "Positive Belief."

If you did, you would make that choice based on the belief that your choice will bring you closer to the place you want to be in your life, or to being what you want to be in your life. Remember, that is a goal.

To bring you some clarity around this idea, here is a drawing of it:

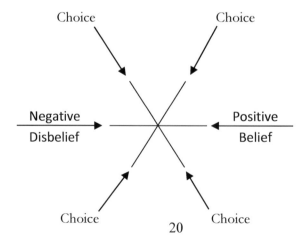

20

Take a look at this drawing. Do you see how in every moment (the middle of the X) you are met with a choice? And do you see how in that same moment, you are met with a belief? Now, look at that moment, and look at the fact that each belief is the basis, or the foundation, for the action you take.

Every action you take is going to lead you to a new moment, and the pattern will continue.

The more often you make choices, based on negative disbeliefs, the more often you may get what you don't want. The more often you make choices based on positive beliefs, the more often you may get what you do want.

Here is an example of the pattern. Do your best to write on the chart and fill in the parts. It will really help you to understand all of this. The more you understand it, the more you will be able to create the exact life you want!

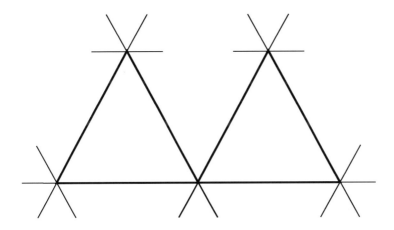

Did you name each part of the pattern? Good!

Do you now see how each moment comes with the opportunity to have a new belief? I'm sure it's all starting to become clear to you now.

The magic of the pattern of life is that it can be altered at any moment. Every moment is an opportunity to choose a new belief. The more often you choose a certain belief, the more solid your belief system becomes.

Now, I said that the more often you choose a positive belief, the more often you MAY get what you want, and vice versa.

Why would I say that you MAY get what you want? Wouldn't you be guaranteed to get what you want as long as your belief is what it needs to be? Nope! Unfortunately, there are no guarantees in life. However, you can increase the PROBABILITY of getting what you want based on your belief system.

Take a look, at this:

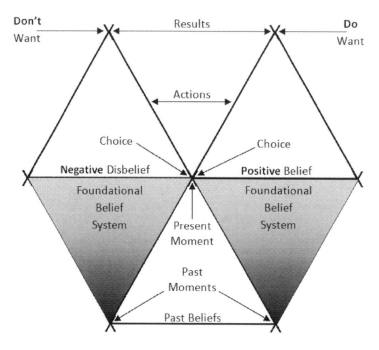

If your life has been full of negative disbeliefs up until this point, what may be showing through in your life today are your layers of past beliefs. The longer you have been believing something, the more difficult it can be to change that thought or belief and have a new way of being show through for you. This image might help you to understand :

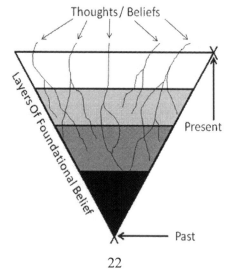

Thoughts and beliefs in the present moment always show up as new. Simply because this is a new moment, and how you choose to show up is up to you. However, changing those beliefs, so they show up as YOU want to show up, takes intentional focus on being the way you want to be, thinking the way you want to think, and believing what you want to believe!

This might be what you have experienced in your life.

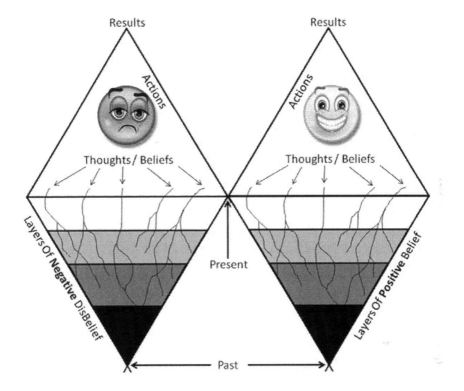

If your actions were taken on a foundation of negative disbelief, your results will be one thing, if they were taken on a foundation of positive belief, your results will be another.

Neither belief guarantees your results, however, let me ask you a question. "If the determination of whether or not you got the result you wanted was based on your thoughts, which of these would you choose?

Would you choose to take action on layers of negative disbelief, or layers of positive belief?

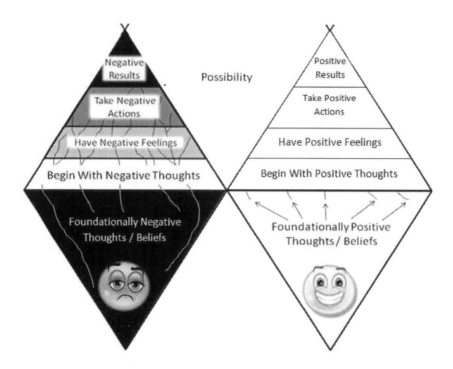

I would guess that if the results of your thoughts and beliefs, resulted in the actions you took, and then you were guaranteed a positive result, you would work really hard on building a positive foundational belief system.

Here is the issue.

Outside of EVERYTHING ELSE is something that cannot be controlled. It is at the center of everything, and exists for its own purposes. That is POSSIBILITY!

Possibility is what decides what happens. We make the choice, we take the action, possibility decides the result. Possibility allows life to happen the way it should happen. Possibility allows us to enjoy choice, and experience life. Possibility is what makes life exciting!

Possibility lives here

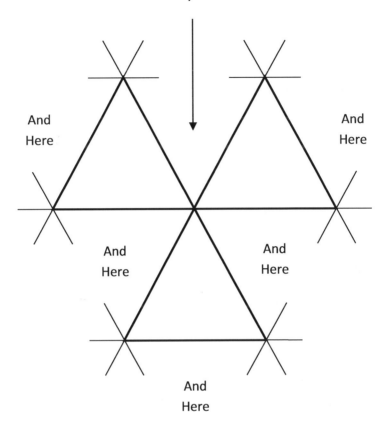

And Here

And Here

And Here

And Here

And Here

Can you see where possibility exists? It exists in our belief system!

If you are feeling overwhelmed by all of this, take a break. You are learning some very advanced concepts here! Don't give up! This will help you live the exact life you want to live, I promise!

You will completely understand this stuff by the end of the book! If your eyes are glazing over like a donut right now, it's because your brain needs time to absorb the information. You may need to live life and think about these patterns in order to fully grasp the idea. Once you get it, you will have an Ah HA moment like no other.

It's amazing, once you fully understand what I am talking about, how you will literally be able to relate every single aspect of your life to what is in this book. There will not be one single thing that occurs in your life, that you will be unable to link to what you are learning here.

I don't want to lose you because I'm getting a bit more technical. This information matters, because if you get the meaning of this, you will get life itself!

10

What Happens...... Happens

There is a very real fact to all of this. What happens, happens. It just does, it just is. Whatever you choose to BELIEVE in the moment "it" happens, is what will cause what happens next.

What I mean by that is, just because something happens once, does not mean it will always happen. The same way that just because something doesn't happen once, does not mean it will not happen the next time.

However, there is one factor that helps in the determination of the result. That is the probability factor.

The probability factor is what you can use, to make a logical conclusion based on what you believe will happen. There is still no guarantee, however, you increase the probability by making the appropriate choice, taking the appropriate action, and doing both, based on the positive belief that if you do what needs to be done you will be able to get what you want.

Based on everything I've been saying so far, what do you think the most logical thing to do would be?

Would it be a good idea, and make sense to live every moment of life, with a positive attitude, based on a positive belief, and make good choices that lead to good actions? Of course it would.

SO WHY DON'T PEOPLE DO IT?

It's because this type of education is not part of the mandatory education you receive in school! Don't ask me why. I guess the smart people who determine what you are supposed to learn, don't think this is important enough to include it in every school in the world....YET!

I am personally determined to make this book part of the mandatory curriculum for early life, in every possible place, across the globe!

That's not the focus of this chapter though. The focus of this chapter is to introduce you to the word YET!

Yet, yeT, yET, YET! Kind of a funny word if you say it over and over.

If anything is possible, and even based on your previous results, you don't necessarily believe it's possible, does that make it not possible? No, it just means it hasn't happened, YET!

So if at the beginning of the ABC's of Success book, you made an agreement with me, and yourself, that you would not give up, then what is a great word to use in your desire to achieve your goals?

YET!!!!

This might not be standard education, YET!

This might not be the book that helps change the world, YET!

This might not be the information that educates a new generation of free thinkers who use this information to improve the entire way of life as we know it, YET!

But it can be, because I believe it's possible!

Now let me ask you a question. Based on what you have learned so far, what is possible for your life?

What is the story that you want to write for your life?

What do you want to believe?

What actions do you want to take?

What results to do want to have?

It's up to you!

Right now, in this very moment, you have the ability to alter the entire course of your life! You know the pattern, you just have to master using it!

You might not have the exact life you want, YET, but isn't it possible that if you keep going, and keep making choices, and taking actions based on what you believe in, that you may someday be living the exact life you want to be living in the world that you created?

Absolutely!

So any time someone tells you that you can't do something, or that you probably won't do something, don't give up based on their probability factor. If it matters to you, and you believe it's possible, then go for it! If you are willing to put in 100% commitment, all the effort it will take, and you are able to accept the result, no matter what happens, then do it!

If you fail once, great! You are one step closer to a possible success! If you fail twice, awesome! Another lesson learned in what NOT to do!

The best is YET to come for you! Create your life, based on the possibility that you can be anything you want, and the probability factor that others have done it many times before you!

This is your life, you get to decide the probability of you being a huge success, very famous, extremely wealthy, or anything else you want to be.

Increase the probability factors and the possibility of you being a major success is HUGE!

11

So why don't people

Why don't people live the lives they want to live?

First and foremost I believe it's because they don't know the same thing that you do now. You are learning something now, that most adults have never learned.

The reality of the world is that it is the product of this pattern. People have been weaving together moments, based on beliefs, and taking actions without having any intentional purpose for their life for generations now,

I'm out to change that! I'm on a mission to create a new GENERATION X!

I want to create a generation of thinkers who believe that anything is possible. If the moment is the center of the X and in the moment, anything is possible, then being generation X would mean that you are part of a generation that can indeed change the world, based on what YOU believe is possible!

I want you to OWN BEING GENERATION X and BE THE GENERATION OF POSSIBILITY!

X = Possibility !

Once you understand what that means, you are going to want to stand up for that possibility! For now, just remember, that you can be anything you want to be in this world, and it all starts with the belief that you can be.

I believe you are an endless generation of possibilities with more resources at your fingertips than any generation before you.

You are able to do what has never been done before! Now, I need to show you why!

12

Choose your Way Of Being

If you want to re-write the story of the world, it has to start with YOU! You are the most important person in your life, and you are the most important person in the world!

Since I'm writing this to everyone in the world, the same goes for everyone!

Everyone, everywhere, is the most important person ever born! We…. Me and You, need to start treating them, and ourselves, that way!

This moment is the most important moment of your life. And since the same goes for everyone, then this moment is the most important moment in everyone's life.

If everyone is the most important person in the world, and every moment is the most important moment, then what matters right now, and what matters from this moment on?

EVERYTHING MATTERS! And EVERYONE MATTERS!

If that is true, then how are you going to start being in your life? Are you going to be the person who sets the example for others to follow? Are you going to lead people on the path toward the belief that everyone and everything matters and in this moment. Are you going to be conciententional, because how you are being matters?

I hope so!

I need to warn you of something though. The way you are being exists is a very specific place, at a very specific time. It's the peak of what is possible in our world, and it only exists in one place at.

The warning I need to make is that on either side of that place, at every moment, is the darkness.

In this very moment, you are surrounded by the possibility of darkness. Luckily, you are also surrounded by light. Since you are focused on the light, that is what you see.

Here is how you KEEP light in your life. You focus on how much you love the light, you focus on being thankful for the light, and you focus on the light at every moment of your life.

Is that completely possible? Absolutely!

Is that completely probable? Not really!

That is because, the darkness is going to use everything it has, to cause you to experience a L.A.N.D.S.L.I.D.E.

13

Desired Envisionments

Imagine a world, where everyone was kind to each other, had what they wanted, and it was as close to perfection as you could possibly imagine.

Wouldn't that be a great place to live!

Literally a place where you were able to look around you and say "This is exactly where I want to be!"

What would it take to create a place like that? It would take a belief that a place like that could actually exist, and it would take consistent, specific, intentional action in order to create it.

That is what I want to teach you how to create right now.

Imagine a specific goal you want to achieve. It could be the achievement of an award, a specific place you want to go, or even something you want to have. It can also be a way you want to feel or be in your life.

Go ahead and envision that place right now, as if you already have it in your life. What does that feel like? Really imagine the environment, how does it look, and what are you experiencing now that you are living in that place.

The envisioned environment is what I call your DESIRED ENVISIONMENT of life.

You see, at all times you either are, or are not being what you want to be. When you are being it, you are living in your DESIRED ENVISIONMENT, when you are not living in your desired envisionment you are having a L.A.N.D.S.L.I.D.E.

Let me ask you something specific. If you could choose to be one thing at ALL TIMES, what would it be?

For me, my answer is joyously loving!

I choose joyously loving, because I don't see another way of being that is more rewarding. Because joy is not the result of anything else in life, it's simply a choice of how I want to feel, and love is the thing that makes all things better.

Regardless of what I want, what do you want to be?

Whatever you want to be living in is your desired envisionment of your life. Even if you just want to be living in the belief that something is possible, that is a desired envisionment as well.

To give you an example, you might want to live in the desired envisionment that one day you will be a world famous singer. Or perhaps you want to believe that you will be a major league ball player. If that is what you want to be, that is what you BELIEVE.

Since I have no idea what you want to be, I'll use my example of BEING JOYOUSLY LOVING as the example.

If I was creating the desired envisionment of being joyously loving, I would describe that as a place of inner peace, where I chose to love everything about my life, despite what might be happening in my life. Even if there is chaos, arguing, or some other circumstance that could hold me back from being joyous, I will still BE joyous. Even if there was fighting, I would still be loving.

Is that easy? Not at all, but it's a choice of how I'm choosing to be in the moment.

In order for me to live in that place in my life, I would have to have the positive belief that it's even possible.

So let me ask you. What do you want to be? What desired envisionment do you want to live in? Make the choice and live there NOW!

Your desired envisionment is the place just above the dark clouds of fire. Remember the F.I.R.E. we talked about in The Next Level? The Fears, Influences, Reasons, and Emotions!

∧

This space above the clouds of
F.I.R.E. is your Desired Envisionment

F.I.R.E.

This area is where you live
when you L.A.N.D.S.L.I.D.E.

14

Landslide

If your desired envisionment is where you want to live, then what would cause you to live somewhere other than where you want to be?

That would be a L . A . N . D . S . L . I . D . E

Landslides happen when the darkness creeps into your mindset, and makes you start living a negative disbelief that your desired envisionment for your life isn't possible.

Remember, the darkness loves it when you are living below the dark clouds of F.I.R.E. where it can hurl insults at you because it knows you feel smaller than the fears, influences, reasons and emotions *it* wants you to believe are possible in your mind at that moment.

That darkness, and its weapons against you begin to show up as thoughts in your mind, because of a story you begin to believe. When those thoughts begin, the very foundational belief system you have begins to shake. You begin to lose your footing. You might fall down, feel like you are failing, mess up, say the wrong thing, do the wrong thing, and before you know it you are sliding.

You are slipping and you can't seem to gain any traction. It's like the ground below you is crumbling and you are falling toward that dark place you just climbed past!

Oh no, what is happening? You just overcame these things, and now you are heading back to where you don't want to be. You do your best to grab onto anything you can that will help you stop, but it's all sliding with you.

This is a LANDSLIDE!!!

This is how it happens. Each moment you have a choice of believing that you either are where you want to be, or are not where you want to be. You have the choice of believing that you can be where you want to be, or you can doubt it.

When you begin to have a **N**egative **D**isbelief about what is possible, and you stop having positive beliefs, the landslide begins. Before you know it, you are face to face with the darkness and it's spitting at you and telling you to give up!

Your NEGATIVE DISBELIEF, stopped you from living in your DESIRED ENVISIONMENT!

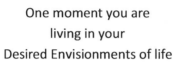

One moment you are
living in your
Desired Envisionments of life

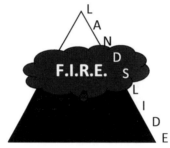

Something happens
that causes you to
LANDSLIDE

Landslides happen when you…..

START
Living
A
Negative
Disbelief
STOP
Living
In
Desired
Envisionments

When your mindset begins to fade from the light of possibility, to the darkness of despair, you keep sliding, and sliding and sliding until you do one thing.

Let's figure out what that is right now.

15

The dark and the light

The light is what gives you all things good. The darkness is what desires to destroy all things good.

The best way to continue to receive the good things in your life, is to continue to focus on the light.

THE LIGHT POURS ALL GOOD THINGS UPON YOU!

Here is what you must realize. The key to getting more of what you want in life, is to focus on being thankful for the good things you already have.

Let me give you an example. If you give someone a gift, and they are very thankful for the gift you gave them, does it make you want to give them more? Of course, when someone is appreciative of what you give them, it naturally makes you want to give more.

So if the light is what gives you all things good, then you need to show the light ALL the appreciation for what you get in the world.

At any given moment, you should be focused on the light, and when you want to show your appreciation for anything you have in your life, the best way to show that appreciation is to raise your arms up high above your head and out to the side.

If you do that right now, you'll see that the position you take, looks like a funnel. This allows you to funnel the entire energy of the universe into your heart. Take a deep breath, smile a huge smile, and give pure thanks for what you do have.

That can be anything! Your health, your friends, your family, your skills, your ability to even read this is a gift. As you continue to grow up, begin to offer more thanks and appreciation to the light of possibility for all the good things you have in your life.

The more thanks you give, the more the universal light of the universe wants to give you back.

The opposite occurs when you are facing the darkness. When you are working hard to save yourself from having a landslide, your arms are down and you are funneling in to your head, only what is below you.

Only one universal force can save you from a landslide. The Light!

16

How to stop a landslide

Now that you know that landslides are caused when you start living **a** **n**egative **d**isbelief and **s**top **l**iving **in** **d**esired **e**nvisionments, the big question is "How do you stop a landslide?"

Again, like most of what you are learning, it's not always easy, but it's really simple.

A landslide is one of the most devastating natural forces in the world. It starts with one movement, and as the earth begins to crumble and slide in a continuous chain reaction of pressure, it can bury people, demolish houses, and destroy everything in its path.

Mental landslides can be the same, and do the same thing. If you are having a mental landslide, you can find yourself destroying everything in your path! When It begins, it might just seem like a few small negative disbeliefs. Then all of the sudden, you are stuck in it, and you seem to be unable to get away. Before long, your life feels out of control, and you feel like you are the victim of life, and of your circumstances.

On the way down, you are reaching for and grasping at anything you can hold on to, but none of it seems to be doing you any good. You continue to lose control, and the more you do, the faster you begin to slide!

Now, before you take out everything and everyone in your path of destruction, I want to show you a simple way to stop a landslide.

Just give up control! Allow yourself to stop trying. Instead of grasping for something else to stop your life from spinning out of control, just stop for a moment.

Stop, take a breath, and look up. Raise your arms up high and funnel the light into your body. Allow nothing to be wrong, even for just a second, and just surrender.

What is happening, is happening. There is nothing wrong, everything just is as it is.

What happens when you stop, raise your arms, and give up control? You give up trying. When you give up trying, you begin doing what you need to be doing, which is BEING in the moment.

I'll illustrate this with an example:

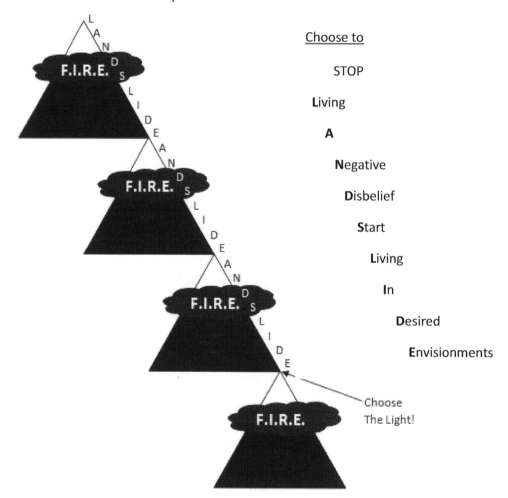

The moment you choose to stop living a negative disbelief, you START living in your desired envisionment. The moment you stop living in the darkness, you start living in the light.

At that exact moment, you land somewhere very special! You land in the exact place you are supposed to be, at the exact moment you are supposed to be there. You land at the peak!

The peak of life is where you are supposed to live, at all times! It's actually where you DO live at all times. You can only be in one place physically, however, mentally, it can feel like you are anywhere you choose to be.

Landslides happen when you think things should be the way they are not. You focus on the past, or you focus on the future. Things may not be exactly the way you want them to be right now. I understand that, however, they are how they are, and in this moment you can either accept that, or have a landslide.

So the way you stop a landslide is to STOP living **a negative disbelief** & START living **in desired envisionments!**

Your desired envisionment is what YOU create. So if you just stop, accept what is happening as a unique and perfect moment in your life that is to be experienced, then you can do something you haven't been doing during your landslide down the mountain.

You can ask for help from the light! The light is the space above you. When you ask the light for help, you have to trust that you will have solid ground to stand on. You have to believe that you are where you are for a reason. The moment you begin to believe that, is the moment you begin living in the light of possibility!

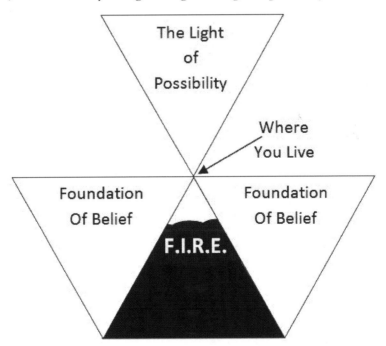

As long as you are living in the moment, you are living at the exact place the light needs you to be. The F.I.R.E. and the darkness can't touch you, because the light holds it back.

45

You see, there are two ways to look at life. You either look at it like you are living in the exact place you are meant to be, or like you are stuck in a place you don't want to be.

It looks like this.

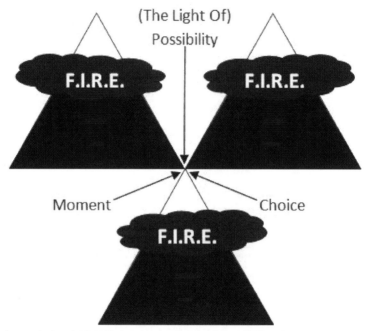

You get to choose! Are YOU living in the light of possibility, in the exact place you are supposed to be. OR, are you living at the bottom of the mountain, stuck below the dark clouds of f.i.r.e?

Whenever you are experiencing an emotional breakdown, and what you are feeling is not how you want to be feeling, it's because you are starting to landslide.

This can, and does, happen in all of our lives. In order to stop the landslide, you need to choose how you want to feel. Then, once you choose how you want to feel, just stop for a minute. Understand that the way you are feeling is the result of living some sort of negative disbelief about the way you believe life should be.

The reality of your life is that it is what it is. The only way to improve it is to use what you have learned in this book to make positive change.

If you are intentionally living your life in the way YOU want to live it, then nothing and no one can cause a landslide but you.

In this, and every moment, it's your choice!

17

Using The LIGHT

So how do you use the light? How do you get to the point where you are able to use the light at any given moment, so you can begin to enjoy life more, at every moment, and stop having landslides of negative disbeliefs?

You are already at that point! Right now, in this very moment, you are in the exact place you need to be in order to use the light of possibility to help you be, do, and have anything you want in your life.

There is a reality to our lives, and if you can realize it now, you will be far ahead of many other people. You are, right now, exactly where you need to be in order to live the exact life you want to live!

I believe that you are always in the exact place you are supposed to be. If you weren't, you wouldn't be there. I also believe that every moment of your life serves a purpose. It may seem insignificant to you at the time, but each moment, no matter how boring or challenging, is meant to teach you something.

When you call upon the light of possibility, at any time, you can rest assured that you are being heard. No matter how dark it may seem at the time, the light is just one moment away. All you need to do is seek it, call upon it, and use it to help you through each difficult situation.

Here is what I mean. The darkness is able to cover your life and pour down all the fire it wants upon you, as long as you are living below its influence. Since you get to choose where you are living, in the light, or in the darkness, you get to choose what you see.

Every single moment of your life, you get to choose whether you want to be living in the darkness, or living in the light. It's just a matter of changing your perspective and your focus. The light, is always there for you!

The Light Of Possibility
Pierces The Darkness
And Meets You
Everywhere
You Need
It To
Be

As long as you are looking toward the light of possibility, you will not be living in darkness.

The light is there to teach you, and to help you see what needs to be done in every moment. The light is there to guide you through each difficult time. The light is a lamp to your feet and light to your path as you journey toward your destiny.

Any time you need the light, you just simply raise your arms high in the air and ask for help. At those times where raising your arms isn't appropriate, just raise your eyes, lift your heart, and give your worries over to the light. When you do that, the darkness will fade away and the landslide will stop.

18

Now That You Know

Now that you know how to use the light of possibility to help guide your life, how do you use this information to help you live the life you want to live?

The reality of your life is that you have to make the choice that this exact life you have right now is the life you want to live, first. If you aren't choosing to be happy, you aren't going to be happy. Happiness, living in the light, and everything else you do in life is a choice.

Don't get me wrong, I understand, especially as a young person, that sometimes things happen that are beyond your control. In fact, everything is beyond your control. In the reality of life, you don't control anything.

You do, however, have the ability to influence everything!

As long as you are living at the peak, which is where the light meets your life, you are living at the highest place possible! When you live in that place, you are only being influenced by one thing, the universal light. It's the only thing above you!

If you learn to put your trust in the light of possibility, you will begin to understand why anything is possible in your life. The light of possibility wants to pour down upon you, everything in its power, and help you flood the world with what you want to see.

Imagine yourself, literally standing at the highest peak of the highest mountain top in the world. If you were there, and you asked the light to pour down upon you anything you wanted to see in the world, then you would be the person touched by what you want first. After you have what you want, it would continue to pour over you, and begin to flood the world around you.

Anything you are given is a gift. The universe is able to give you anything you want, and more than you could possibly imagine. You just need to be specific about what you ask for, be open to receiving it, be patient in its delivery, and be willing to share your gifts with the world. Most importantly, you need to be thankful, beyond what most people would consider enough thanks, so that the universal light sees that you appreciate what it is doing in your life.

When you are willing to share what is given to you, and thankful for the opportunities placed at your feet, you show the universe, which is the creator of all things, that YOU ARE ALSO A LIGHT OF POSSIBILITY! The sun may be the brightest light, however, it uses the rest of the stars to shine when it needs them too.

Take a look at this and imagine it is your life. In this picture, you are like a bucket. You are funneling in the light, and you are asking for exactly what you want in life. As long as you are doing what we talked about, being specific, open to receiving, patient, willing to share, and most importantly, thankful for what you receive, the light will continue to pour upon you what you ask for.

Your energy that you give off is like a force field around you. If you are giving away gifts of love, understanding, friendship, knowledge, goodness, and other positive qualities, you will flood the world with what you have to offer. You will be able to literally influence the entire world!

You must begin to create something called an "Abundance Mentality!" An abundance mentality is created when you believe that you will have more than enough. When you live abundantly, you openly share whatever you have for the benefit of others. By believing you have more than enough, and sharing what you have, you show the light that you are able to handle more and more.

Any time you get something good, give thanks! No matter how small or insignificant it might seem to you. What you focus on, expands! So if you find a penny on the ground, be extremely thankful for finding that penny! It was placed in your path, and your focus was brought to its attention.

When you show thanks for even the smallest gifts, the people around you, and even the universe itself wants to give you more and more!

Try it out! See if I'm wrong about this. Give yourself one month of pure thankfulness of everything you have, and see what changes in your life.

19

Uh Oh!

Uh Oh! In case you didn't know, this works the other way too! If you are not living in the light, and you are living in the darkness instead, you will do the same thing.

Your energy force field is a constantly flowing and all consuming way of being that is able to flood the world around you. You take in what you are surrounded by, and you filter it through yourself, and back out into the world.

So what happens if you are living in the darkness? What happens if you are looking at the world and believing that it's full of hate, nastiness, unkind words, misunderstanding, and nothing good? I'll show you....

You overflow with F.I.R.E. and the darkness fills your life.

F.I.R.E.

Your Fears, Influences, Reasons, and Emotions flood the world around you.

You

The World

Just as you can receive and take in the light, you can also receive and take in the darkness. When you do that, your energy becomes a dark, negative energy that people can feel.

Let me bring one more thing to your attention. If you are surrounded by people who live in the darkness, what energy do you think you are being flooded with?

Take a serious look at who you spend your time with. Who are your closest friends? Are they the type of people who live in the light of possibility, or do they tend to live in the darkness?

Ask yourself, "Why am I spending my precious time with these people?" If you don't like the results you are seeing in your life, it may be a result of the flood of negativity you are experiencing from the people you are standing next to.

Choose your friends wisely. It's been said that you are the average of the five people you spend the most time with. If those five people don't have what you want, then you need to start spending more time, around the people who do have what you want.

Do you like to be around people who are full of dark, negative energy? I don't!

The energy you give off is a direct result of what you are choosing to focus on. If you choose to focus on the belief that you can't have something in your life, then guess what? You will be getting exactly the thing you are focusing on.

If you stand in the light of possibility and ask the universe, the creator, the light, or whatever else you want to think of it as, for exactly what you want, you can receive it!

20

The science behind it

There is actually some really cool, very specific science behind all this. You can look into it, and find out that a lot of what I'm saying is actually scientific fact! The rest of it, I began to understand out of my own life experience and from that understanding, I created the pattern of life design…..

The reality of energy is that it works in something called a Torus Vortex. A torus vortex is a really cool looking shape. In fact it's the basis of all energy in the world. It looks like this.

The energy is produced in the center, it flows down around you, floods the world, and

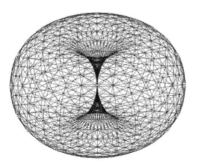

comes back upon you. It's a continuous cycle of energy.

I'd like to put all this together for you, and then show you how to use all of it to help you design the exact life you want to live! Sound good?

Okay, so you already learned that X is the basis of all possibility. So I want to go ahead and place the X of possibility as the starting point of the Torus Vortex. Ooooohhh, Mr. smart guy is using big words now!

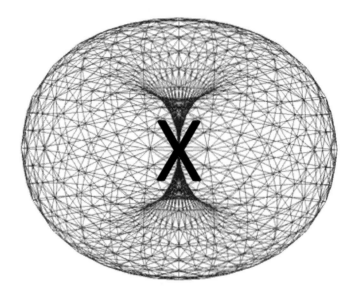

If the X (possibility) is placed at the same point as the beginning of all energy, then what is the cause of all energy? X is! If you are a light of possibility, and you believe that, then what is going to flow out of you? The light of possibility flows out from within you, out around you, and back into you.

You become the source of all energy. In this example, you are generating X, which makes you the ultimate generation X.

Take a look at this.

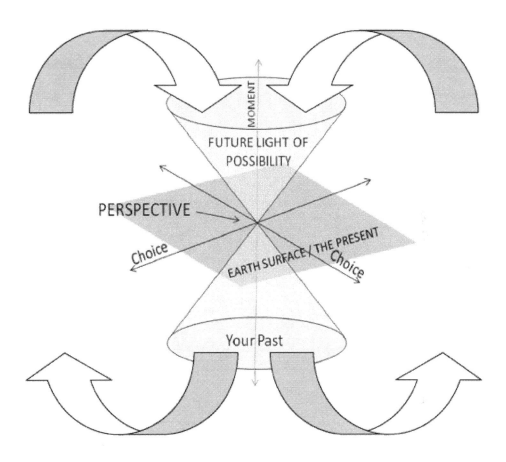

If how you see things (Your perspective) is what generates your energy, then let me ask you something. How are you going to CHOOSE to see life from now on?

If X is the moment, and X is also a choice, and to top it all off, X is also possibility, then what are you?

You are X! You are the determining factor in the equation of your life! How you choose to see life, is how life shows up for you!

I believe that you are X because I believe that you are possibility itself!

21

What is possible

So if you are the determining factor in what is possible in your life, then what are you going to believe is possible in your life from this point on?

I would hope that you would say that you are going to believe that ANYTHING is possible! If anything is possible, then what could you know for sure, without ever opening up the possibility for something else? Nothing.

From now on, if you are going to be a light of possibility, and you are going to be the determining factor (X) in the story of your life, then you must believe that all things are possible.

If you agree that all things are possible, then who can be right? Anyone! If you agree that all things are possible, then who can be wrong? No one!

So if it's true, that based on the science of how energy is created, in a torus vortex, that starts with X, then from now on you would have to believe that you are the beginning and the end of what is possible in your life and in the world.

If you are the beginning and the end of possibility, and you, and no one else can be right or wrong, then what are you left with?

BELIEF!!

Belief is the only thing that determines your ability to make something possible in your life.

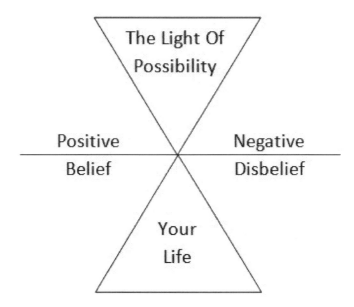

Belief is the very sensitive scale that tips things in your favor or not. Belief is what moves your life in a particular direction!

From this point on, if you begin to develop a very strong belief system in the fact that anything is possible, you can move your life in any direction you want it to go!

What do you want to believe is possible for your life? If based on what I've been showing you, it's all just a matter of what you believe, the actions you consistently take, and the time it takes to reach the peak, then doesn't that open up the doors to amazing possibilities in your life?

Heck yeah it does!

So now that you understand, and hopefully believe, that anything is possible in your life, we get to have some fun designing it the way you want to live life!

This is my favorite part!

22

The design process

When a designer designs something, they typically start with a simple idea, and as the idea becomes more clear in their mind, they increase the details. Each new idea improves the designers ability to refine the idea and improve it even more. Many ideas, for instance, the toothbrush, have been modified thousands of times. Each design improves on the last design and what is possible, even with a toothbrush, is endless.

All it takes is some imagination, a desire to make something happen, and the action. The result is a new design.

The same goes for your life! If you want to live the exact life you want to live, and be whatever you want to be, then you will need to start with the broad description of what you want your life to be. We are going to start doing some exercises to help you, design your life!

Before we begin, I want to ask you to do one thing for me. HAVE FUN! Life is supposed to be fun! If you aren't having fun, you aren't doing it right! Anything can be fun if your perspective of it is that it IS fun.

I promise, I am going to make this fun.

Let me ask you, what do you want to be in your life? I know that is a broad question. Seriously though, what do you want to be?

Do you want to be, happy, rich, famous, well liked, in a great relationship? What do you want? I literally want you to just let go of the belief that something isn't possible in your life. Just let your ideas flow, and write down what you want to be now, some time in the future, and maybe just as a distant dream.

The same goes for what you DON'T want to be. What don't you want to be in your life. Do you not want to be unhappy? Do you not want to be poor, unknown, unliked, and in a bad relationship? That is important too! You have to understand what you don't want to be, in order to recognize when you have that.

Let's do it. Let's begin designing your life!

In this first exercise, I want you to take a look at the following page and see that on the left side of the page is the phrase "I want to be." On the right side of the page is the phrase "I don't want to be."

Under each column, write down anything. Literally anything. Whatever you want to be, whether it's right away, or whether it's just some distant possibility, write it down. Be sure to write down what you do, and don't, want to be.

Here is an example of how that might look.

I want to be	I don't want to be
Earning money	Broke
Dating Frank/Michelle	Not dating anyone
Rich and famous	Poor and unknown
Healthy	Unhealthy
An astronaut	Stuck on earth
A dog owner	Petless
Driving in six months	Begging for rides
Loving my job	Hating my job
Listened to / heard	Ignored / unheard

It's your list, so make it what you want it to be. Just let it flow, and don't think about how something would happen, just have the desire to BE it right now.

Make sure you phrase it so that it always reads "I want to be….." or "I don't want to be…."

This is important as you'll soon find out.

GO!

I want to be   I don't want to be

AWESOME! You have literally just done more than most people have ever done in the planning of your life. Many people don't live the life they want to live, because they simply don't plan their life.

Now don't get me wrong, just because you plan it, doesn't mean it's going to go exactly as planned. This is life after all. It's unpredictable, surprising, and just when you think you have it figured out, it throws you for a loop. That's the fun of it!

Let me ask you a question though. Is it easier to get back on track if you have a plan or if you don't have a plan? It's obviously easier with a plan.

So that is what we are going to do. We are going to plan your life, to the best of your ability, so that you create your life and live the way you want to live, instead of doing what most people do, which is to have no plan, and allow life to dictate what happens to them.

23

Now what

Now that you have written down what you do and don't want to be in your life, we're going to do something really fun!

Take a look at that page you just wrote on. In the center is a line. The line separates what you do want to be, from what you don't want to be.

Fold that page along the line and keep creasing it back and forth so you can tear it easily. Once you have it creased, go ahead and tear that page in half and completely remove what you don't want to be from this book. Hold on to that list of things that you don't want.

Ok, I want you to really be able to focus here. So go to a quiet place where it's just going to be you. Give yourself some space and time to begin designing your life!

Are you there? If not, go! This is important!

Now that you are literally holding in your hands, everything you don't want to be in your life, I want you to begin looking at that list.

Really take some time and imagine each of those things. If you don't want to be unhappy, then really imagine yourself being unhappy. If you don't want to be broke, then really imagine yourself living your life, completely broke. If you don't want to be in a terrible relationship, then I want you to envision yourself waking up each day, dreading the fact that you have to spend one more day with this person, even if you aren't even in a relationship now.

Look at the list. Read it. Imagine that this is your life. In just a few years, it's completely possible that everything you don't want to be could in fact be your real life.

Get disgusted by that idea. Allow your lip to curl, and allow yourself to get angry at the very idea of this life being your life. Get completely bothered by it. Cry, shake at the emotion of anger, frustration, disgust, and feel it in the depth of your body! This is how your life can be!

I hope that you are feeling completely disgusted by this list. I hope you are literally ready to scream and even throw up at the thought of this being your life. This is what you need to imagine in order for your emotions to be one of the very things that keeps you from ever living in the darkness.

Right now, in this moment, you might even have some of these things. Let that bother you!

Now, if you are at the point where you want to destroy this list, that is what I want you to do. I want you to tear it up, shred it, flush it down the toilet, or anything else you can do to safely, and deliberately get rid of this list. Get it out of your life, forever!

DO IT NOW!!!!

24

That feels great

Doesn't that exercise feel great! Doesn't it feel amazing to get rid of what you don't want in your life! Heck yeah it does!

The reality of life is that we let in to our lives what we choose to let into our life. Sure, things we don't want can show up for a short time, however, it's your choice of whether to allow it to stay there or not.

From now on, unless you CHOOSE to let what you don't want back into your life, you've officially removed those things!

Now that you have gotten rid of all the things you don't want to be in your life, I want you to look at the list of what you DO want to be in your life.

Take a look at that list, and imagine your life when you have all those things! The reality of life is that you are either living the life you want, or you are not living the life you want. You are either BEING what you want to be, or you are NOT BEING what you want to be.

So as you look at this list, ask yourself, "How can I be this in my life?"

The simple answer is that you need a plan, you need to follow that plan, and you need to improve upon the plan as the design of your life becomes more clear to you.

I'm going to help you design a really fun, really simple plan, for anything you want to be in your life! Cool rightLet's get started!

First, go ahead and pick one thing on your list that you want to be, and that you believe you can be immediately. This will probably be an internal way of being.

For instance, you might believe that you can be happy, motivated, focused, loving, or any other feeling. Go ahead and choose one and write it here.

I want to be _____

Now that you have something you want to be, I want you to design your ABC's of success plan. Let's start with the B, since that is the foundation of everything. I'll use the example of "I want to be motivated!" If you want to be that, then what do you need to believe? You need to believe things like "I believe that I need to accomplish what I want to accomplish quickly." Or, "I believe my goals are extremely important."

So what do you need to believe?

I believe _____

I believe _____

I believe _____

What actions do you need to take in order to BE that? If your goal was to be motivated, you could say "I need to wake up each day, excited by my reason why." Or, "I need to focus on what matters to me in my life."

So what do you need to do?

I need to _____

I need to _____

I need to _____

How consistently do you need to do those things? "Every morning when I first wake up." Or, "Every time I am wasting time."

How often _____

How often _____

How often _____

Hey, you're really good at this stuff!

25

Your inside J . O . B .

Who's JOB is it to be what you want to be in your life? It's your J.O.B! It's your Journey Of Being!

Your journey begins right now, in this moment! For the internal feelings of life, like happy, motivated, inspired, loving, grateful, thankful, beautiful, handsome, funny, creative or anything else, that is a choice!

Your job, is to make an intentional choice of how you are BEING in each moment of life. The way you are being is how you show up. How you show up is the role you are playing and the role you play determines how the story of your life is being viewed.

Let's take it back to the basic design.

If emotions, and ways of being are a choice, then who and determine how you are feeling in your life? You do.

If you determine how you are feeling in your life, then where can you live, emotionally, at all times if you choose to? You can live at the peak, where your desired way of being is!

So if your desired way of being was to be happy, then you would design your life like this.

I want to be

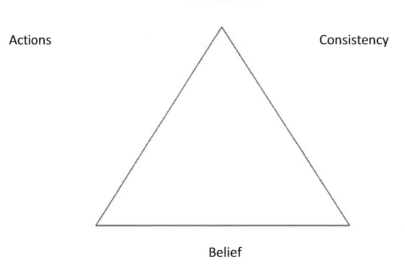

Actions   Consistency

Belief

What actions do you need to take to BE happy?

What beliefs do you need to have in order to BE happy?

How consistently do you need to take the actions and have the beliefs in order to BE happy?

All inside JOBS are a choice of how you are being in the moment. It's not always easy to get the job done, however, it is really simple. If you are feeling unhappy, really upset, even completely emotionally overwhelmed, it's because you are BEING unhappy, BEING really upset, and BEING completely overwhelmed.

When you are being something, you are focused on it. Which means in the case of being unhappy, really upset, and completely overwhelmed, you are focused on what is making you feel that way.

In order to accomplish your goal of being happy, you would simply need to change your focus. Easy? No! Simple? Yes!

Change your focus from what is making you feel the way you do, and begin to focus on what will make you feel the way you WANT to feel.

If you just broke up with your boyfriend or girlfriend, obviously you could focus on being unhappy about that, really upset about that, and completely overwhelmed by that. You could focus on the feeling of being alone, not good enough, like you'll "never" find someone…. OR

You could focus on the fact that you are now free to really put your focus on being with exactly who you want to be with. Or, the fact that maybe the universe is moving you toward someone better for you. Or, that dating is supposed to be fun, and not a constant battle for attention.

You get to choose what you focus on! What you focus on, expands! Choose to focus on what will make you be what you want to be.

.

26

Your Outside JOBS

Outside Jobs are designed the same way, they are just slightly different in the fact that you probably don't actually have the thing you want right now.

If it can only be obtained by specifically doing certain things over time, then the only difference is the moment. You either do have it, or you don't have it, during a specific moment in your life.

For instance, if you want to be working for a particular company, then right now you are at the bottom of the mountain, and where you want to be is at the top of the mountain.

I'll give you an example. My daughter, Taylor, really wants to work for Disney animation studios. Right now, she is at the bottom of the mountain on her climb toward actually working there.

What she needs to do, in order to BE working for Pixar, is the ABC's of Success. She needs to take the right actions, she needs to believe she can do it, and she needs to consistently do both for as long as it takes.

Once her consistent actions and her beliefs meet up at the time in her life when that happens, she will have reached the peak!

This design is the same, for any outside "JOB" (Journey Of Being) that you want in your own life.

I want to be

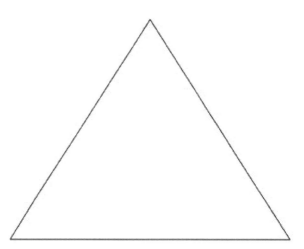

I am here now

The actions, beliefs, and consistency of being what you want to be is all the same. The only factor that changes is TIME!

If you do the ABC's of success, designed around what you want to be, it's going to eventually be yours, unless you either give up, run out of time, or make the choice, after taking action consistently, that you really don't want that particular JOB and you alter your plan to fit the new goal you have chosen for your life.

The plan, the design, the way you go about getting ANYTHING in life, will not change. It's a simple pattern, and the only thing that changes is the specific thing you want to be, and the size of the pattern.

Makes sense right?

27

The Blueprint

Have you ever watched a movie where someone is planning to steal something from a bank, or a museum? They usually come up with a great plan, they draw it out, plan it to the last detail, and obtain a blueprint of the building.

Of course, I'm not suggesting that you do anything like that. I am suggesting that you go about getting what you want in the same way though!

I want to teach you how to draw a blueprint for your life goals!

It's going to take YOU, being a good COP. It's going to require you to create your own LAWS, and it's going to require you to kick out the IMPOSTERS who want to steal your goal away from you before you have it! You're also going to need to be courageous and fight FIRE! If you are willing to do those things, I'm willing to say that you can live a life that is better than your dreams!

Are you up for the task?

GOOD!

First, what is a blueprint? In the design world, a blueprint is a detailed drawing of exactly how something will be built. It would allow for the duplication of a building, or a product, so that it was built the same way every time.

Obviously, since life is going to be different for everyone, and since life is not a duplicatable process because each moment changes, we wouldn't be able to replicate results perfectly every time.

However, wouldn't it be really cool if I showed you a way that you could plan for anything you ever wanted in your life, and with as much certainty as life provides, you would know that by following the plan, you would get what you want?

I THINK THAT IS AWESOME!

What I'm going to introduce you to is the life blueprint. I have to tell you though, that name is pretty boring!

So I'm going to name it

THE PLAN OF AWESOME!

·28

Like A Boss

If you are going to have a J.O.B. in life, you are going to need a boss! Let me ask you, are you able to be a boss? Do you think you have what it takes to get the J.O.B. done?

Let's think about it. What does a boss do? A boss is the one who knows what needs to be done. A boss makes sure the work is done, when it needs to be done. A boss makes sure you show up, when you need to show up. A boss pushes you to get the work done, even when you don't feel like it. A boss doesn't accept excuses, and they expect you to do your best at all times.

Have you ever heard (I'm sure you haven't said it) the statement "You're not the boss of me," when someone is asked to do something? Maybe a parent, teacher, or someone else who is acting as an authority figure wants something done, and that statement is thrown back at them. That's not a good thing to say!

You are the boss of you! And if that's true, you better act like it! Those people are looking out for your best interest and want you to understand what it's like to have a boss. Bosses can be demanding! So if you are going to be the one to create your life, you are going to have to demand the best of yourself at all times. It's pretty hard to look in the mirror and say "You're not the boss of me!"

Are you ready to be your own boss? If so, you are going to have to be your own source of motivation. You will need to make sure that you show up, and do what you need to do in order to get the J.O.B. done. You need to allow no excuses from yourself, and you will need to do your best at all times.

If you are willing to do that and more, for yourself and others, then I think you have what it takes to work for yourself. From now on, you will be self employed in your own J.O.B. and you will be responsible for your own success and even your own failures.

Now that you have agreed to be the boss, the worker, and the person responsible for your life, it's time to get started on your plan of awesome!

Now get to work….. LIKE A BOSS!

29

The Plan Of Awesome!

In the plan of awesome, you are going to think of anything that sounds awesome to you, and make a plan to have it as your life! In fact, you already have a plan started. That list you made, which has all the things you want to be on it, is the start of your plan of awesome!

It's only the beginning though! Your plan of awesome is going to change throughout your life, which is why using this book, and not just reading this book, is going to make a huge difference in how AWESOME your life is!

First, you need to understand that everything you wrote down on your list, is a desired envisionment of life. It's something you want to be and it's where you want to live. Remember, if it's an inside J.O.B. then it's simply a matter of choice for you to have it in your life. It's still going to require a plan of awesome though, because life has a way of seeming not awesome at times.

The plan of awesome goes like this. You start out as a boss, you hire yourself for whatever J.O.B. you want, and you decide when the work is complete and it's time to move on to another J.O.B.

As the boss, you hire yourself to write the LAWS of your desired envisionment.

In order to enforce the laws, you will need a COP. You must also hire yourself to be the COP. As a COP, it's your job to help people live in your envisionment, or use your influence to get them to leave.

Of course, you will need a vehicle. As a boss, you don't just drive any old CAR, you drive something with muscle! I'll tell you what you drive in just a bit.

You also get to decide what an IMPOSTER looks like. When you recognize an imposter, inside your envisionment, you must get rid of them or help them live by your ways of being.

Finally, you will need to be a FIRE fighter, and use your vehicle to blast through to the other side, where it's nothing but blue skies and possibility!

Are you wondering what all this means? If so keep reading, it gets awesomer!

30

Your new life

In your new life, which is the life you live from this moment on, you will be forced to make some tough choices. The choices you make will determine the outcome of your life. Rest assured, when you make your choices, based on what you want for your life, you will look back and see that you lived life on purpose!

The first thing I want you to understand about living life in your desired envisionments is that you must be the driving force in that life. If you want something, YOU must be the one who makes it happen.

So let's start with the vehicle you should drive when you want to reach the peak. What do you think you should drive? Personally, I suggest a freight train!

When you drive your life in a freight train, you become unstoppable. You lay down a clear track, and you become the person who blows the whistle and let's everyone know YOU'RE COMING THROUGH, SO LOOK OUT!

The most important thing to driving a freight train to the peak is to be sure you don't weigh yourself down with too many goals. Attach a single goal to your engine and get moving toward the peak right away!

Any time something falls in front of you, on your track to success, you need to push it to full power and blast through whatever stands in your way..... LIKE A BOSS!

Becoming unstoppable is all about mindset!

So let's begin learning how to design Your Plan Of Awesome!

First, what is the one Desired envisionment you want to live in, more than anything, right away? Go ahead and name it. If you want to be happy, then your desired envisionment is called "Happy." If you want to be confident, then you live in the desired envisionment of confident.

I live in the desired environment of

_____

Understand something! I didn't have you write down where you wanted to live, I had you write down WHERE YOU LIVE!

You need to OWN your desired envisionments of life!

Even if the envisionment is something you are working toward as an external desire, like being a video game designer, an artist, or the captain of my team, you must OWN THAT BELIEF!

In that case it would say "I live in the desired envisionment of being a video game designer!" Or, "I live in the desired envisionment of being the captain of the team!"

You must own your envisionments!

Since you own the place you want to live, you get to make the LAWS! The L.A.W.S. are the people and things that **L**ive **A**nd **W**on't **S**urvive in your envisionment.

So if you live in the envisionment of being happy, what won't survive there? Unhappiness, negativity, foul language, lasting disappointment, are the types of things that won't survive in that envisionment.

You also need to decide what Lives in your envisionment of happy. Other happy people, supportive people, positive people, kind words, enthusiasm, might live in your envisionment. You get to decide!

Be sure to keep your laws in line with the envisionment. You can own as many envisionments as you want, so don't have rich people in your envisionment if they aren't happy. Trust me, not all rich people are happy people!

Go ahead and write down what Lives And Won't Survive in your desired envisionment.

Lives	And	Won't Survive
_____		_____
_____		_____
_____		_____

Once you have developed a strong set of LAWS, you must enforce them. It's very important that if negativity won't survive in YOUR envisionment of life, that you do everything you need to do to remove it from your life. This might mean leaving the place you are in, not being around certain people, not watching certain shows, not reading people's social media posts, and more. It's all about making the choice to not allow something into your life, or your desired envisionment.

Why do LAWS matter? What is the purpose of LAWS? What are laws?

LAWS are a specific set of rules, set in place to protect an environment, which are enforceable by penalty.

The penalty for breaking your laws is that you might have to remove that person or thing from your life. No drama required! If something breaks your laws, you simply enforce the penalty to protect your environment.

What are those things that might break the laws? I like to think of them as "IMPOSTERS!" Imposters love to hold you back from making something POSSIBLE in your life. An imposter might say "That's not possible!" or, they might say, "I've tried that, don't even bother."

However, imposters can also be objects, places, or anything else.

An IMPOSTER - "IMPEDES POSSIBILITY!"

If something is holding you back from getting to where you want to be in your life, it's an IMPOSTER! When imposters live in your envisionment, they do their best to cause a LANDSLIDE! Well, truth be told, the only one that can actually cause a landslide is you. Because, landslides are beliefs, and only you can have your beliefs. It may seem like it's the fault of others, however, if you blame them, you are playing the blame game. To blame in life is to BE LAME!

So in order to enforce the penalty of your laws, what do you need to be? You need to be a COP! What does a COP do? A COP does two things. They enforce the laws by removing the imposter from a situation, or by helping restore peace in life.

If you are going to be a COP in your envisionments of life, you are going to need to remove the imposters, or help the imposters to live by your laws, in order to restore peace.

But what gives you the right to be a COP? A COP, in your envisionments of life is the Creator Of Purpose! The C . O . P . (Creator Of Purpose) is the person responsible for deciding why this matters. So what is the purpose of your envisionment?

Is the purpose of your envisionment of being happy, because you recognize that negativity and unhappiness hold you back from being who you want to be? Great! That is a purpose!

Is the purpose of your envisionment of being rich one day, because you want to use your money as a way of helping other people, including yourself, live a better life? AWESOME! That's a great purpose!

What is the purpose of your envisionment? You get to create it, you get to enforce the laws, and you get to do what it takes to restore peace.

You restore peace by either removing the imposter, or by helping the imposter to live in the envisionment you have designed. It's up to you to decide which of the two options to choose.

If you live in the envisionment of happy, and you see someone sad, it's your J.O.B. to remove them from your life or help them live in the envisionment of happy. I don't recommend being too quick to just remove things from your life. If you do that, you will begin to alienate yourself from the world around you.

It's best to learn how to help others work and live within your envisionment of life. Just because someone is unhappy, or negative, doesn't mean they want to be that way. So in order to live in the envisionment of happy, without just living alone at the top of a mountain and being happy, you should help others learn to be that way too.

That might mean that you add a positive comment to a negative social media post, or that instead of going along with the crowd that is being mean to someone, you choose to be friends with that person instead.

By doing this, for yourself and for others, you begin to create the world in the way you want to see it. Be that change you want to see in your life, and eventually you may see that change in the world around you.

31

Break it down

I'd like to teach you a simple method of figuring out how to achieve the REALLY BIG goals in your life. This is important because most people envision HUGE possibilities for themselves, yet they often get overwhelmed and do nothing toward the achievement of that goal.

I'm going to teach you to turn your goals upside down and view them from a new perspective too! You know, this whole book, I've encouraged you to think of goals, your life, and the achievements of your life as a mountain of success. The problem with that is the fact that you might not be ready to climb the HUGE mountain you created for yourself.

So if that is the case, and even if it's not, here is a great way to take a really big goal, and break it down into smaller "Peaks" so that each accomplished goal, leads you closer to living the exact life you want.

Look at this picture

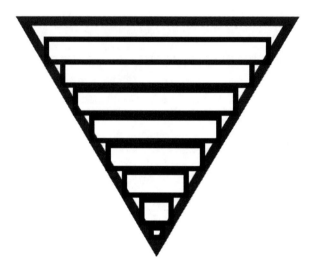

It's the exact same shape as the mountain, except it's facing the opposite direction. Instead of each step being something you have to climb, each step becomes a smaller and smaller task that needs to be completed so that the large goal fits into your life.

A lot of times we jam a giant goal into our lives in an attempt to achieve something great! The problem is, just like a funnel, if you attempt to jam something too big into it, the thing won't flow.

Life is like a river. It's supposed to flow. Even a giant river starts out as a trickle of water and turns into an unstoppable force that is able to flow over, around, through, and powerfully overtake whatever stands in its way.

So begin thinking about your goals like you would begin filling a bottle with a funnel. Break down your large goals, into smaller pieces, and get them flowing in your life.

32

Bullseye

The fact is, hitting your goals is an important thing to do if you want to live a more rewarding, successful, fulfilled life. Every person is going to have different goals for their life, and each of us have a different view of what "Success" looks like.

In target shooting, the highest point value is the bullseye. If you can successfully hit the center of the target, more than anyone else, you win. This is how I want you to think about your goals.

Take a look at this picture.

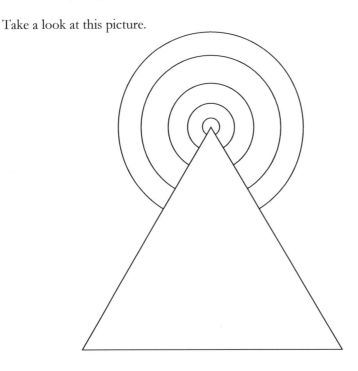

Does it look like a mountain, with a bullseye? Does it also look like a light, shining upon the mountain top? If your goal was to hit the very center of the target, this would give you a clear indication of where you need to aim, right?

This just also happens to look like the cover of the book, doesn't it. AHA! Now it's all starting to make sense, right!

I want you to think of this as your map of how you want to live life. On your journey of being, ultimately, you want to be at the peak, in the center of the bullseye.

In life, and in this moment, the peak of the mountain is exactly where you are.

What I also want you to think about is how that image looks like a light, radiating out from exactly where you are. At the center, the light is completely focused, and all around the center is outgoing waves of light that continue to expand, forever.

From now on, in your life, I want you to embrace this image as the design of your life. It's everything we've talked about up until this point. That bullseye, that light, that mountain, all represent YOU!

You are everything that picture represents! You are a light, you are focused, you are success, you are the most important part of your life, you are exactly where you should be.

The most important thing I want you to take away from this entire book series is this statement.

"I am, a light of possibility, in this moment, I choose to be…."

That statement is my life statement of purpose. You are welcome to use it as your own, or come up with your own. Let me explain what that statement means to me.

I am - I am who, what, and how I am! No one else can say the same thing and make it mean what I make it mean!

A light - As a light, I cannot be stopped, contained, defined, or held back forever. I can however, concentrate and be as focused as a laser, or radiate and be an all consuming force in the world around me.

Of Possibility - Possibility, like light, can be anything you want it to be. You can be focused on the possibility or you can allow it to be out there, waiting for the right time for it to become reality.

In this moment - Right now, this very second that you are reading _this_ word, is the very moment I am talking about, and it always will be.

90

I choose - I get to use the greatest gift that's ever been given to me. I get to choose, based on nothing but what I want.

To BE - Who, what, and how I am being is what I send out into this world. What I send out, starts as a focus point, and radiates out, affecting this world in ways I will immediately see, and in ways I will probably never know.

…….. - This is the most important part of the entire statement of purpose.

The ………. Is the purpose.

"I am, a light of possibility, in this moment, I choose to be ……"

I get to say that, first, and whatever purpose I put into the …….. is the way I am being in the world.

"You are, a light of possibility, in this moment, what will you choose to be?"

33

It's all a journey

It's all a journey. How you choose to reach the final destination is up to you. You can rush through life, unfocused on the moments, or you can slow down, enjoying each and every finite moment as it happens.

How you live your life is not for me to decide. It's for you to choose.

Your journey is happening right now, as a young person, and it will continue, until you are a little older. It will also keep moving until you are a lot older, and it won't stop because you want it to. Your journey, is your time on earth. How you choose to spend your time on earth is up to you.

I would like to give you some personal statements that I believe will help you along your journey. The more often you get used to saying these things to yourself, the better. I recommend even printing them out, framing them, and hanging them on your wall.

They are called "Mantras" and you can make them mean whatever you want them to mean. Use them to propel you forward toward the life you want to be living. Here we go…..

DECLARE THESE!

I believe I am the designer of my life. Whatever I envision for my life is possible. There is a purpose for my life and I am committed to identifying and living that purpose at every moment.

I believe that my future is mine to direct and I must not allow fear, reasons, influence, or negative emotions to stop me from living the life I envision for myself. I am the biggest and most powerful force in directing my life.

I believe that opportunity is all around me at every moment of every day. I choose to be open to those opportunities, I recognize those opportunities, and I take action on those opportunities.

I believe that I do not need the approval of other people to live the life that I envision for myself. If I am going to live the life that I envision for myself, I must create it. I must live in it and only then can I invite people to come and live there with me. I cannot force people to do anything. I can only influence them to take a journey with me.

I believe that there are people who will hold me back and I believe that there are people who will propel me forward. I choose to surround myself with the people who will propel me forward toward the life that I want to live.

I believe that my thoughts are the most powerful force in my life. I am fully aware of my thoughts at all times and I choose to focus on the thoughts that empower me.

I believe that having a strong connection with the people who will propel me forward is one of my greatest and most valuable resources. I choose to connect with people who have the same values and the same vision that I have for my life.

I believe that every moment is an opportunity to learn. The universe is constantly providing me with the information I need to succeed. I am always open to this information.

I believe that I have the ability to overcome any block that gets in my way of success. I am aware of the fact that fear, reason, negative emotions and influence will be present in my life but I choose to break through those blocks with power.

I believe that I have nothing more than this present moment. I know that I cannot change my past and I also know that in order to create my future, I need to envision what I want and take actions right now, in this moment. As long as I make choices aligned with my purpose, my actions will propel me toward the life I want to live.

I believe that my actions are the determining factor in my success and that The Light of possibility will allow me and help me to have everything that I want in my life as long as it suits the greater purpose of the universe.

I believe that I can successfully fail and when I fail that I am making progress. I know that the only way to not succeed is to give up completely. I choose to keep going no matter what gets in my way. I will mess up but I will not give up.

I believe that my life is an ever-evolving space of possibility. Possibility can be shaped and improved at any time to benefit my life and help me to live the life that I want.

I believe that I should be thankful for what I have in my life but that it's okay to desire more. I am on this earth to live a life of complete abundance. It is my desire that keeps me reaching for new levels of possibility but it is my thankfulness that brings me inner peace in the moment.

I believe that I have everything I need to succeed within me. I have the ability to attract anything that I want into my life and the ability to make it my reality.

34

Circles of possibility

When you design your life, you don't have to know exactly what you want. As you begin to intentionally design your life, you will begin to gain clarity of exactly what you want through the natural design process.

As your clarity intensifies so will your light! As your light intensifies, so will your focus on exactly what you should be doing at each and every moment of your life. The tools you have learned to use within this book should help you to begin designing your life, more strategically than most of the rest of the world. That is, until my goal of the entire world reading this book becomes a reality.

If you want to be a standout, a superstar, a person who lives their life with the intentional purpose that you were born to live it with, then I have great news for you! You are going to start aiming for the bullseye of your life right now!

I'm going to use a technique I call "Circles Of Possibility." In this technique, you are going to start placing your life goals in specific areas of life, so that you know how much energy you should be putting into them. Each circle is going to begin from this moment, and expand out from the present, into what could simply be a distant time from now.

The reality is this. If you begin now, to write down your personal goals, and identify what you want to be in your life, you are far more likely to live that life and achieve those goals!

So look at the Circles Of Possibility chart. It looks like a bullseye target. In the center of that target is where your present moment is. It's the most important thing you can be working on. As the circles expand, so do the possibilities! I don't want you to hold anything back, if you can think of it, put it in a circle. Even if that circle is so far out that simply wondering how it could ever be possible begins to stop you from writing it down, WRITE IT DOWN ANYWAY!

I personally believe that the universal light of possibility makes all things possible. What may seem impossible to you, is possible with the light, if what the light wants is something it makes matter.

You've seen that my drawing of the Torus Vortex of how our lives are created looks like this:

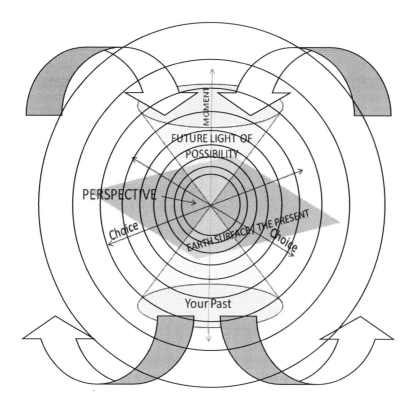

That just also happens to be how science illustrates the creation of matter and the theory of relativity. Look it up!

I know it's an advanced concept, however, it's also a pretty amazing realization once you really understand it!

Basically what I'm saying is that with "The Light" all things are possible. It's just a matter of whether or not the light is concentrated on making it possible.

As you fill in your circles of possibility, fill in the circles depending on how close to the present moment reality you want them to be. If it's relatively possible, put it in the outer rings, if it's a distant possibility, put it all the way to the outside. If it's something you see as possible within a short time, put it closer to the center. If you want to make it not only possible, but a REALITY, then place it at the very center. Most of all, focus your light, and allow the universal light to focus too. Be crystal clear in what you want, and do what it takes to make it your reality.

This is called the "Circle Of Possibility" exercise. In each of the circles on the next page, write in what you want to BE. The most immediate goal should be right at the center of the bullseye, and your more distant, long term goals should go toward the outer rings. You can even use the far outside to list things that you may ultimately want to be some time in your lifetime, but know that it's a distant possibility and something to work toward in your lifetime.

This is how MY circles of possibility might look. These are things I've declared that I want to be…..

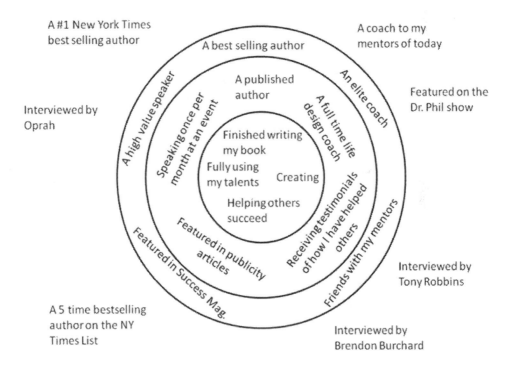

Now that you have some things you want to focus on, you can design your life around exactly what you want. On the following pages, you're going to find some "Plan Of Awesome" worksheets that will help you to fill in all the details, and give you a blueprint of how you want your life to be!

As you accomplish goals, move the outside possibilities to the center circles. Do this in pencil if you want (recommended) and use this book as your guidebook for creating and living the exact life you want to live!

As you accomplish immediate goals, you can move the outer goals into the center so you can really focus on making them the reality of your life, instead of just the possibility!

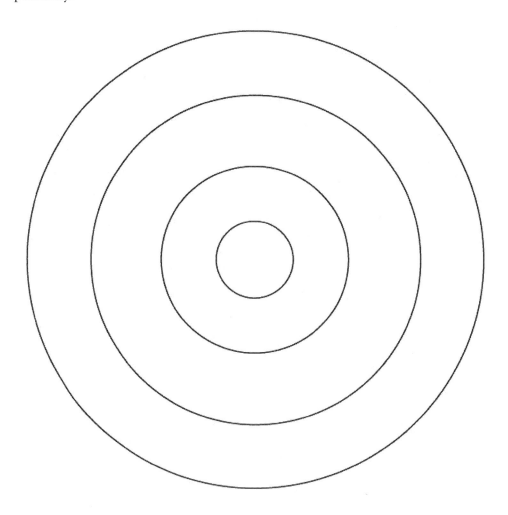

35

The design

The design of life won't change. It's a pattern. The size of the goal determines the size of the pattern. If you have a BIG goal, make a detailed, specific pattern that keeps you on track. If you have a little goal, make a little plan to keep you on track.

The worksheets on the following pages are designed to help you design your life goals, and ways of being, so that you have a blueprint of exactly how to go out into your world and take what it has to offer you!

Just fill in each section. Start with what you will be, write it in. Then fill in the ABC's. Be sure to acknowledge the F.I.R.E. that might get in your way. Describe the purpose, create your laws and identify what imposters might show up so you are ready to deal with them.

Most of all, have fun with this!

MY PLAN OF AWESOME!

In my Desired Envisionment

I will be

My **A**ctions will be: **C**onsistently (when) I will do it:

F.I.R.E.

I **B**elieve:

I am the **C.O.P.** of my envisionment and here is why it exists.

_____

_____

These are the L.A.W.S. of my envisionment that I will enforce.

Lives   **A**nd   **W**on't Survive

_____   _____

_____   _____

_____   _____

Imposters may show up in my envisionment and try to make me

_____

_____

MY PLAN OF AWESOME!

In my Desired Envisionment

I will be

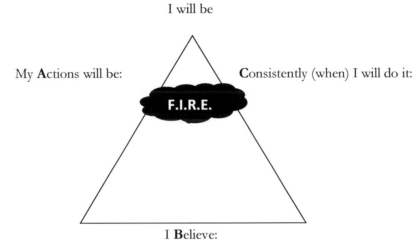

My **A**ctions will be: **C**onsistently (when) I will do it:

F.I.R.E.

I **B**elieve:

I am the **C.O.P.** of my envisionment and here is why it exists.

_____

_____

These are the L.A.W.S. of my envisionment that I will enforce.

Lives   **A**nd   **W**on't Survive

_____   _____

_____   _____

_____   _____

Imposters may show up in my envisionment and try to make me

_____

_____

MY PLAN OF AWESOME!

In my Desired Envisionment

I will be

My **A**ctions will be: Consistently (when) I will do it:

F.I.R.E.

I **B**elieve:

I am the **C.O.P.** of my envisionment and here is why it exists.

_____

_____

These are the L.A.W.S. of my envisionment that I will enforce.

Lives   **A**nd   **W**on't **S**urvive

_____   _____

_____   _____

_____   _____

Imposters may show up in my envisionment and try to make me

_____

_____

MY PLAN OF AWESOME!

In my Desired Envisionment

I will be

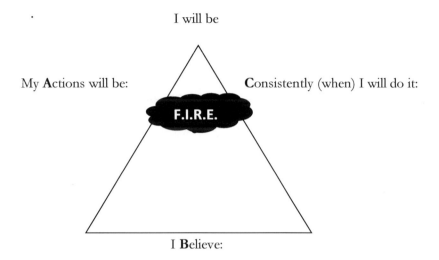

My **A**ctions will be:

Consistently (when) I will do it:

F.I.R.E.

I **B**elieve:

I am the **C.O.P.** of my envisionment and here is why it exists.

_____

_____

These are the L.A.W.S. of my envisionment that I will enforce.

Lives   **A**nd   **W**on't Survive

_____   _____

_____   _____

_____   _____

Imposters may show up in my envisionment and try to make me

_____

_____

MY PLAN OF AWESOME!

In my Desired Envisionment

I will be

My **A**ctions will be:

Consistently (when) I will do it:

F.I.R.E.

I **B**elieve:

I am the **C.O.P.** of my envisionment and here is why it exists.

_____

_____

These are the L.A.W.S. of my envisionment that I will enforce.

Lives	**A**nd	**W**on't Survive
_____		_____
_____		_____
_____		_____

Imposters may show up in my envisionment and try to make me

_____

_____

36

Life at the PEAK

You've finally reached the envisionment of possibility! I'm so proud of you for reaching this point! It's not easy to read a big book of words, but it is simple. Just like the way to the peak is step by step, the way to read any book is word by word.

As a final place of rest, where you can raise your arms in victory, knowing you have reached the point where it all makes sense to you, there is the peak.

At the peak, life just exists. You have everything below you, and nothing but a space of possibility above you. You can see life from every perspective your eyes allow, and in that space, you are truly being YOU!

But what is the peak? The peak is this moment. The peak is every moment. The peak is what you stand upon when you refuse to have a landslide and you choose to live in the light.

When you live at the peak, the light, and the foundation of everything you have ever experienced all come together. Right now, this exact moment in your life, and forever more, you are living at your peak. If you choose to be!

As you know by now, I LOVE acronyms! The P.E.A.K. is no exception. It's an acronym for how to live life. Let me help you to understand.

P = Perspective…. Your perspective is the way you see life. It's not however, the way life happens. It's simply your view of it. When you live at the peak, you can see life from every perspective. Learn to view life from every possible way. Understand that everyone has a perspective, and the more you can learn to see life the way THEY see it, the better you will be at adjusting what you need to be, and do, in order to have what you want.

If life isn't happening the way you want it to be happening, Ask yourself, "What is another way I could look at this situation right now?"

E = Expectations…. Your expectations are YOUR expectations. They are a future issue. If you are living your life, in an expectation, you are not living your life in the present moment.

Give up expectations of life!

Life is going to happen the way life is going to happen. As long as you have clear desired envisionments that you want to be living in, you can adjust who, what, and how you are being, and what you are doing, in the moment, to suit your needs and wants. Your mind will be much more clear and able to make the right choice when you stop living in a "What if?"

If life isn't happening the way you want it to be happening, ask yourself "What am I expecting to happen?"

A = Awareness…. An awareness of who, what, and how you are being is very important to living life in the moment it is happening. Being present, and being aware of whether or not you are truly living NOW, is not only going to improve how you adjust to life. It's also going to have a profound impact on the quality of how you live life.

Being aware of the possibilities all around you will allow you to make split second choices that are in line with what you want to be. The more aware you are of yourself, and others, the more present you will be.

Be aware of the fact that the present is a gift!

If you are living in the past by focusing on what was, or living in the future by focusing on what if, you miss out on the present gift of what is.

If life isn't happening the way you want it to be happening, ask yourself, "What am I not being aware of?"

K = Knowledge….. Knowledge is not just the stuff they make you learn in school. Knowledge is your ability to understand that which you currently do not. Life is an ever evolving space of possibility, knowledge is never ending as well. Seek out knowledge!

By seeking out knowledge, you seek to understand something that is not yet understood.

If something is confusing to you. Ask questions! Be curious!

Most importantly, ask the right people! If you want the answer, go to the source of the information. Always seek **know**ledge from the one who knows.

If life isn't happening the way you want it to be happening, ask yourself, "What do I need to understand more?"

Then go and seek out the knowledge!

The reality of life is that anything is possible when you believe it is. So don't be a know it all! Be a believer in what's possible.

When your desire is to know it all, and to be right, you stop asking questions and you make life wrong.

When you live life at the peak, you live in a space of complete possibility. You live your life the way it was intended to be lived, in the moment, joyously aware of the fact that the light of possibility is shining brightly upon you at every moment.

All you ever need to do is look up, ask the all knowing to guide your way, and allow the light to show you the way.

37

What matters

What matters in life? Before I answer that, let's look at what "Matter" really is.

Matter is everything. In scientific terms, matter cannot be created or destroyed, only transformed.

So in your life, everything matters. However, at the same time, nothing matters.

Literally everything matters. Every moment matters, every word matters, every thought matters, and everything, every one, everywhere, every time, all matter. Since it all matters, and matter cannot be created or destroyed, only transformed, then you need to transform what matters into how you want your life to be.

At the same time, nothing matters. Literally nothing. I say that because nothing is the matter. Nothing is wrong. Everything just is. What you are experiencing is the matter at hand. Nothing is wrong with matter, matter just is.

What I mean by "Nothing Matters" is that unless you make what is happening in your life "Wrong" then it's just right. Many times we find ourselves looking at our lives as if it's supposed to be something it's not. Your life is what it is, and unless you choose to make it seem wrong, then it's just perfect. You are exactly where you are supposed to be, and what is happening is exactly what is supposed to be happening in your life. It's all a learning experience.

In order to make the matter (your life) right, you just need to accept the matter (your life) as it is happening. If you desire to make the matter different, then transform it to suit your needs.

What's the matter with life? Everything is the matter with life, and nothing is the matter with life, because life is matter!

What's the matter with your life? Everything, and nothing is the matter with your life, because how you view, live, and experience your life matters!

You, yourself, are matter! You are made up of matter, and you cannot be created or destroyed, only transformed. One day, you were transformed into who you are today. One day, you will transform into whatever we transform into when we leave this earth. What you do with this transformation you are experiencing right now, during your lifetime, matters!

It matters to the world! It matters to the people around you! It should matter most of all, to you!

Who, what, and how you want to be in this world, during your time in it, matters!

Be what matters to you! Be what matters to everyone else too!

Start looking for WHY you matter, and transform yourself into that reason.

If you don't know why you matter, ask the people around you. If they won't tell you, Ask the light of possibility! Isn't it possible that the light of possibility placed you in the exact place you are in right now for a reason? If you believe anything I've said, up until this point, you would have to say yes.

Look for the lesson in every moment!

It's also possible that there is no reason for it all. It's possible that we are just evolutionary creatures who are born, live, and die with no purpose.

I don't believe that for one second though. I believe that right now, we are in a transitional space of possibility. This moment, this choice, and this possibility that your life matters is what I believe.

No matter what you believe, I have to tell you one simple thing. This entire book series, every word of it, is completely made up. It's made up of what I believe. Beliefs, like matter, cannot be created or destroyed, only transformed.

If you want to believe that what I've said is true, that's great! If you want to believe that what I've said is not true, that's great too.

None of it matters anyway, because this book is just about finished. It doesn't matter if you believe me or not, because life is just going to happen anyway. Personally, I believe that there is so much truth in this book that it must be believed.

What does matter, is whether or not you believe this book matters. If this book is something you want other people to read, then share it with them. The only way people gain knowledge is by understanding that which they do not already understand.

If you see someone living anywhere but the peak from now on, suggest this book series to them. Say "I used to feel that same way. I read a book that completely changed my perspective. You might like it!"

Whatever you do, don't ever tell anyone that they NEED these books. People don't like to be told what they need, they like to be told what they might like.

When someone asks what the book is, tell them, it's Your Journey OF Being A Teenager, and it's my J.O.B. to tell you about it!

Whether or not you share this book matters.

You probably won't get paid for sharing this book, but you sure will be rewarded if everyone in this world reads it and begins treating you like you matter.

38

The light of possibility

I believe there is a universal light of possibility, shining down upon us all, at every moment. I believe that light guides our life, and each step we take is a reflection of whether or not we are living in the light, or the darkness. I believe that the universal light of possibility wants me to live the exact life I want to live, as long as it doesn't destroy the overall purpose the universe has for my life.

I believe that the light of possibility that guides us all has given us the power of itself, and that power is to shine! We are a reflection of that light, and what we believe is possible is nothing compared to what the light of possibility can actually show us is possible.

These are just my personal beliefs. I don't actually know if anything I've written in this series is true. I personally believe it's all true and it's some of the most needed information in the world.

You have to decide if what I've taught you, makes sense to you. You have to decide whether or not this pattern of life is the pattern by which you will design your life.

I am just like you. I am just a regular old guy, doing his best to live the best life I can. To me, teaching other people how to live the best life they can, to be a light of possibility as a reflection of THE light of possibility, is my ultimate purpose on this earth.

I have chosen this to be my personal design of life. I am a life design expert, and I do my best to expertly design my life around what I want to be. You can be a life design expert too, it's actually a really cool J . O . B .

My hope is that you will find something within you, that gives you the passion, courage, and ambition it takes to succeed at the highest levels possible in life. Only you can decide what level that is for you. When you live in the light of possibility, you can begin to see new possibilities in every moment. When you are open to receiving the messages that the universe is sending to you, your ability to live the life you want to live will be an inspiration to others.

It's my hope, that you will be a light of possibility for others at all times. If you fall off track or have a landslide, just stop, gather yourself, and recommit to being who, what, and how you want to be. You already are where you are supposed to be!

I hope you choose early in life, WHY you are the way you are, and you make it matter to you. You are who you say you are, so be careful when you say "I am….." Yet, even if you have been what you thought you were, and in this moment you choose to be something new, then choose it and BE it.

I believe that you have a very specific purpose on this earth, and I hope that I have helped you to understand what that might be. By choosing your purpose, you give your life purpose, in every moment!

Don't just look for your greatest purpose in life, look for your purpose in each and every moment. Make every moment matter and give every moment a purpose!

Is your purpose in this moment to be kind, loving, supportive, caring, understanding, giving, or a friend to someone who needs one?

Is your purpose in this moment to be working on your desired career so that you can be who you were born to be and be paid for doing it well?

Is your purpose in this moment to just be sitting quietly, thinking about how awesomely life is designed, and how amazing it is that you get the choice of who, what, and how you are going to be, and you also get to choose why?

Is your purpose in this moment to be listening, learning, growing, and understanding what the world around you is telling you?

Is your purpose in this moment to be the best you can be, whether you are playing a sport, taking a test, practicing an instrument or something else you enjoy?

What is your purpose in life? I'll tell you right now!

Your purpose in life is to create your life, and to live your life with an intentional way of being that serves this world in the best way possible. How you choose to do that is up to you!

It's with my greatest respect for you, as a young person, that I hope I've gained your trust and belief in me as a mentor, a friend, and someone who can help you live the life you were born to live! If there is anything I can do to help you, please don't ever hesitate to reach out to me via email at Tom@lifetrax.com so that I can offer you support and guidance.

It's my Journey Of Being, to BE a light of possibility in your life!

As promised, I can assure you that your purpose, in this exact moment, right now, is to be finished reading this book.

Made in the USA
Charleston, SC
09 December 2016